S0-BCP-818

Dog Training

Ernest H. Hart

© **Copyright 1991 by T.F.H. Publications, Inc.**

Distributed in the UNITED STATES by T.F.H. Publications, Inc., One
T.F.H. Plaza, Neptune City, NJ 07753; in CANADA to the Pet Trade by
H & L Pet Supplies Inc., 27 Kingston Crescent, Kitchener, Ontario N2B
2T6; Rolf C. Hagen Ltd., 3225 Sartelon Street, Montreal 382 Quebec; in
CANADA to the Book Trade by Macmillan of Canada (A Division of Can-
ada Publishing Corporation), 164 Commander Boulevard, Agincourt,
Ontario M1S 3C7; in ENGLAND by T.F.H. Publications, PO Box 15, Wa-
terlooville PO7 6BQ; in AUSTRALIA AND THE SOUTH PACIFIC by
T.F.H. (Australia) Pty. Ltd., Box 149, Brookvale 2100 N.S.W., Australia;
in NEW ZEALAND by Ross Haines & Son, Ltd., 82 D Elizabeth Knox
Place, Panmure, Auckland, New Zealand; in the PHILIPPINES by Bio-
Research, 5 Lippay Street, San Lorenzo Village, Makati, Rizal; in
SOUTH AFRICA by Multipet Pty. Ltd., P.O. Box 35347, Northway, 4065,
South Africa. Published by T.F.H. Publications, Inc. Manufactured in the
United States of America by T.F.H. Publications, Inc.

Contents

Color photography: Isabelle Francais,
Ron Reagan, and Vincent Serbin.

Whether you teach your dog to perform tricks or to obey on command, the principles of training are the same: conditioning the animal through repetition to respond in certain ways and rewarding it each time it completes a particular task correctly.

Prologue to Training

The purpose of this book is to train you to train your dog in the quickest and easiest possible way. But before we begin to discuss the actual process of training we must first understand the fundamentals that are the basis of all successful training. In other words, you must understand the *"why"* before the *"how"* so that you will know the reason for the action you perform in order to get a specific result.

There are many degrees of canine training, but first and foremost is fundamental or basic training. After basic training comes companion dog training for competition; advanced obedience training, which includes trailing and scent discrimination; and there is guard or attack work, this latter training a fundamental part of the basic education given to many imported dogs, especially German Shepherd Dogs which have been imported from the Fatherland where it is called Schutz Hund or "Protection Dog" training. There are also the very special educational aspects involved in gun dog,

sheepherding, cattle driving, police, war dog, sled dog, performing dog, rescue dog, draught dog, commercial guard dog and blind-guide dog training. I mention these latter aspects of dog education merely to indicate how very far specialized training can go. In this book we will be mainly concerned with fundamental or basic training and our objective will be to make your dog a better canine citizen whose behavior will be impeccable in your home and car, on the street, and when visiting.

The Key to Training

The key to all canine training, simple or advanced, is *control,* and control is gained by the master over the dog through the conditioning of the animal's reflexes, which means the molding of the shape of the dog's responses to outside stimuli. For example, if you call your hungry puppy to you with a *"beep, beep"* sound each time you feed him you will be conditioning him to

Prologue to Training

come to you for the reward of food and he will associate this reward with the sound. Later the food can be eliminated but the puppy's reaction to the *"beep, beep"* sound will still be triggered by his conditioned reflexes and he will come running with the enthusiasm as previously when the food reward was forthcoming.

Once you have gained this control over your dog you can, if you so desire, progress through basic training to advanced or specialized training in any field. The dog's only boundaries to learning, under the proper training regime, are his own limitations mentally, physically or genetically, for no single individual of any breed is fitted inherently to cope with all the active branches of specialized training. Of course not many owners possess the qualifications or experience necessary to train their dog for highly specialized tasks. But every dog owner can give, indeed it is their *duty* to give, the dog they own the necessary training to insure their pet's good conduct and

gentlemanly deportment. A dog that is uncontrolled can become a nuisance and even a menace that can bring grief and misery to its owner and tragedy to itself or others.

Consistency and *firmness* are the brothers to *control* and, with this trio of virtues (control, consistency and firmness) established in your own being, you are sure of success in training. Be firm, be consistent, and insist that the puppy obey once he knows what it is you want of him. Never allow him to perform an act contrary to your wish.

Other important elements of training are: keep training periods short, ten minutes at the beginning of training, and lengthen the time as you proceed, but never beyond the time when your pup or dog becomes restless and loses interest; use sharp, short, distinctive words of command and always preface every command with the dog's name to capture his immediate interest; approach the training period seriously and try to schedule it at

Prologue to Training

Short, distinctive words such as "Sit!" and "Up!" are commands that work well.

a specific time each day when there will be no outside interruptions; censure your pup when he doesn't obey; praise and reward your dog when he obeys.

I am not a disciple of drastic disciplinary measures. If your dog loves you, is fairly sensitive and has a modicum of canine intelligence, he can be trained by any owner who follows the directions and suggestions in this book. If your dog does not possess the attributes mentioned, if he either doesn't like you or doesn't care, if he is a canine moron, and if he is completely unresponsive, a clod of no sensitivity, then I suggest you either get rid of him and acquire a new dog (and this answer to the problem I highly recommend), because attempting to train such an animal would require the patience and insight of a saint, and I am not referring to the Bernard breed.

Direct physical punishment should be used for only one canine act . . . if your dog willfully and maliciously bites. He should be immediately and drastically punished and made to understand that this act he has committed is not to be tolerated now or ever. Physical punishment as a general form of chastisement should be avoided. Your dog loves you and wants to please you and is sensitive enough to your moods to know by the sound of your voice when you are displeased. Scold him vocally when he does wrong and praise and reward him when he pleases you. Avoid the use of rolled newspaper (which doesn't hurt, most sponsors say, but just frightens through the sound it makes), brooms, switches, your hand, the leash, or any other implement you can think of to strike with as a form of punishment. Your dog may later react unfavorably. If you strike your dog with your hand, you can make him hand shy; the rolled newspaper can become the basis for his eventual chasing of the paper boy; he will learn to run and hide when ever someone sweeps the floor if you use a broom to strike him with; and the leash will become something to shrink from.

The Teacher

Now let us examine our teacher and pupil and see if a few valid remarks will aid in the training program about to be launched. You, the teacher or trainer, love the dog and are therefore inclined to be lenient. If you are, you will never get the required results from your training. Make your dog perform each exercise with complete

consistency every time. To get this result you must yourself be consistent. You must perform each movement used in schooling and pronounce each word of command or communication in the same manner every time. For instance, do not call your dog to you with the command, *"Brucie, come!"* during one training session and, in the next call *"Brucie, here!"*, and expect the animal to understand and perform the act with alacrity and certainty. Inconsistency confuses the dog.

The most important factor of all is, as I previously mentioned, control. But, to gain complete control over your dog you must first have absolute control over *yourself.* During training, if you lose your temper you lose control. Shouting, nagging repetition, angry reprimand, anger that spills over into physical chastisement, and exasperation that you make evident, all confuse your canine pupil. If he does not obey, then the lesson has not been completely learned or he has become frightened by your

Prologue to Training

behavior. He needs teaching, not punishment. And you, on the other hand, need to take stock of, and establish control over, your own vagaries of temperament. Training time should be a serious yet pleasant time of easy intimacy between you and your dog, a time in which a *rapport* is established that will heighten understanding and make your companionship more of a delight than ever before.

The Pupil

Let us now assess the prospective pupil's intelligence, character, and canine characteristics. His eyesight is not as keen as yours, but he is quick to notice movement. Sound and scent are his chief means of communication with his world, and in these departments he is far superior to you. We must reach him, then, through voice and gesture—and realize that he is very sensitive to quality change and intonation in the commanding voice. Therefore, any given command must have a

definite tonal value in keeping with its purpose. The word *"No!"* used in reprimand must be expressed sharply with overtones of displeasure, while *"Good boy!"* employed as praise, should be spoken lightly and pleasantly. Words, as such, have no meaning to the dog, only the sounds they convey register in the canine mentality.

All words of positive command should be spoken sharply and distinctly, in a special "training voice" that you must develop for this specific task. Preface each command with the dog's name. The first word a puppy learns is the word-sound of his name; therefore, by using his name you immediately catch his attention and he is ready to hear and obey the command which follows. Thus, when we want our dog to come to us and his name is Boots, we command, *"Boots, Come!"*

Referring again to our canine pupil, we must realize that intelligence varies in dogs as it does in humans. The ability to learn and to perform is limited by that intelligence as well as by

Prologue to Training

facets of character and physical strengths. These will affect his willingness, energy, sensitivity, aggressiveness, basic stability, and functional ability. By all this I mean that the sensitive dog must be handled with greater care and quietness in training than the less sensitive animal. Aggressive dogs must be trained with great firmness; and an animal which possesses a physical fault which makes certain aspects of training painful cannot be expected to willingly perform such tasks.

As an example of this last named facet of training we can use the experience of one trainer who had a particular dog of great willingness and easy trainability who nevertheless consistently balked at the high jump. The trainer was puzzled by this strange behavior and could find no reason for it, until one day when he had occasion to take some movie film of his dogs working. When the footage arrived that showed this specific animal reluctantly performing over the high jump, he slowed the film down . . . and found the

answer to his problem. The dog's shoulders were not properly angulated so that when it landed, after taking the high jump, the shoulder assembly did not have enough spring and the animal consistently hit its chin painfully upon the ground before it could recover balance.

Training Limits

There are certain limits beyond which your dog cannot go in his training; or perhaps I should say, beyond which it is ridiculous to attempt to push him. These boundaries are established by his genetically inherited behavior patterns. For instance, it is easy to teach an English Setter to point game. It is what he has been bred for and behind this basic urge to point there are the unnumbered generations of English Setters selected for this trait—back to the time when hunters first saw certain Spaniels pause and point the hidden covey of birds before they were flushed. Man selected for this trait, and the pointing breeds gradually evolved.

Prologue to Training

In most of the breeds you will find a similar genealogy—the selection by man for particular traits that fashioned the breed toward a specific use or purpose. It would not be feasible, therefore, to attempt to train a Pug, let us say to point birds in

Some dog breeds are better suited than others for pointing game in the field.

the field or to do any of the work of a gun dog. The Pug is a pet that is not physically fit for field work. If you wish to train a dog to point, select a specimen of one of the many fine pointing breeds. Likewise, if you want a dog that can be trained to herd sheep, avoid the gun dogs and select from the breeds that have been bred for generations for that specific task. ·

Other Training Tips

Always attempt to end the training period on a happy note with both you and your pupil flushed with the feeling of accomplishment. You will find that your dog will perform one of his lessons with gusto, probably one which fits his behavior pattern, such as retrieving an object and bringing it back to hand, which should be an easy lesson to learn for an individual of the bird dog breeds. To end each schooling period with a sense of pleasant achievement will help both of you to approach the next training session with eagerness.

Both punishment and praise must be administered *immediately* after the dog has performed the act which merits such attention. A dog's, and particularly a puppy's, memory is limited and a very short time after he has engaged in a punishable act he has forgotten all about it. It is best, especially when it is necessary to chastise the animal, to catch him while he is performing the deed.

Prologue to Training

Never begin a training period immediately after your dog has been fed. He will be sluggish and not as responsive as you want him to be. When his stomach is empty he is more eager to please, much more lively, and especially eager for the tidbit which you can use as a reward. This tidbit can be any kind of food that your dog particularly craves; a tiny bit of hamburger, cooked liver, kibbled biscuit, or any of the commercial treats. This adjunct to training should be used when teaching your puppy, but when the dog is older and has advanced in his training, the finest reward you can give him is your praise, through your voice and your caressing hand.

It is best for only one person to train a particular dog. Two or more people working the same dog leads to confusion for the animal and a subsequent lack of sureness in his performance.

Approach the dog's training with the assumption that your pupil is intelligent *and,* if he doesn't seem to be able to understand any of the lessons you are attempting to teach him,

it is because you are not using the correct method of teaching and it is therefore *your* fault, not his. In your mind, establish the idea that the opposite of *"praise"* is not *"punishment"* or *"chastisement."* Instead, think of the counter word as *"correction"*. In other words, you praise your dog for performing, and you correct (*not punish*) him when he errs.

Short of a tome on the psychology of the dog or a study on canine behavior patterns, this that you have read is about all you'll need to know as a preliminary to training. Other than determination, patience, and the correct approach to the problem, which I hope you now understand, you will need a soft leather collar, a light chain choke collar and a long training leash.

Determination is a major factor in training, especially if your pupil is young, for with a sad eye a ten-pound puppy can make a sentimental idiot of a tough, rough, two-hundred pound stevedore. Remember this fact about your wily little rascal when you begin his training.

Early Training

Training begins the instant that puppies in the nest feel the touch of the breeder's hand and hear the sound of his voice. When they are being weaned the breeder generally calls them with either a wordless sound of some kind or by saying *"Come puppies!"* when he summons them to the food which he has brought them. The puppy associates the presence of the human and the sound he makes with a pleasureable experience and comes galloping up immediately when he hears or sees the human.

Some breeders put soft collars, with small pieces of rope attached, on the puppies when they are still in the nest. In the course of their daily play the pups grab the small cords and tug and are thus more prepared for later leash breaking.

After you acquire your puppy or dog, handle him frequently and teach him to stand up at arm's length without moving. This is easy to do simply by holding him up and praising and patting him when he stands correctly, using the word

Training should begin as early as posssible; start when the dog is a puppy.

"Stand!" as you caress him. It prepares him for easy grooming or showing, if he is that good a specimen, or for the *"Stand!"* position in his later training. Teaching the pup to stand, to come when called, and leash breaking him simply prepare him for the general training of the future. In this very early training we try to gently mold the puppy to our will and establish a friendly association which will lead naturally and easily into the more rigid training to come.

"No," "Shame," and "Come"

Our first training chore is to teach the puppy to come when

Early Training

called. To do this we must first make the pup familiar with the name we have selected for him. At every opportunity, when playing with the pup or even when you just stop to momentarily pet him, address him by name. When you are ready to feed him or when you give him a tidbit between meals, always have him come to you even if it is only a step, and call *"Jerry, Come!"* Within a very short space of time any normal dog will answer to his name and come when called, for he associates a reward with the sound of his name and the sound of the word that summons him to you.

"No!" and *"Shame!"* are associated words that must be learned early. They must be spoken in an admonishing tone and in such a way that the youngster knows that whatever he has done to call forth these words is wrong and must not be done again.

"No!" should be used when the pup is discovered chewing on something he shouldn't be chewing on, such as the rug,

furniture, or your best pair of shoes. There is a reason for his chewing, of course. He is teething and it eases the pain in his gums. Also he instinctively knows that to remove loose teeth that must come out to make way for new ones, he must chew on

If your puppy is caught in the act of chewing something that it is not supposed to, a firm "No!" should be used.

something. How do you handle this training problem? Simply by the application of a bit of common sense. Supply the pup with something to chew upon (such as Nylabone® , as described at the end of this chapter). Using the *"No!"* command bolstered by the praising *"Good boy!"* delivered in the proper tone of voice, teach

Early Training

the pup what he can and what he can't chew upon to ease his aching gums.

Often the young and playful pup first begins to play with shoes and curtains and various other items of the household before he realizes it's fun to bite them, too. To avoid this unpleasantness, supply the youngster with toys of his own to play with. A little common sense brought to these early, simple dog problems can save expense and aggravation. In terms of training, think of the puppy in the same way you would think of a child who is too young to reason.

The word *"Shame!"* used in training is generally associated with housebreaking, but can also be used in training the pup not to chew household articles. This command must be uttered with withering disgust.

"No!" will be used throughout the animal's training (or, as a matter of fact, throughout his life) to make him aware, when it is uttered, that he has done wrong or is about to do something wrong.

Housebreaking

This is often the tragedy of the novice dog owner, but with a little knowledge and some patience it need not be as terrible a chore as it is assumed to be. First, let us find out where and when a puppy generally defecates and we will be forearmed with pertinent knowledge.

Dogs tend to defecate in areas which they, or other dogs, have previously soiled and they will go to these spots if given the chance. A puppy almost inevitably must relieve himself directly after drinking or awakening from sleep and within half an hour after eating. Avert disaster by taking him to the place you want him to use immediately. If you are breaking him to go outside, and after you have taken him out he comes in and soils the floor or rugs, he must be made to realize that he has done wrong. Scold him with, *"Shame!"* repeated several times and rush him outside again. Praise him extravagantly when he has taken advantage of the great outdoors. If you catch him preparing to void in the house, a quick sharp, *"No!"* will often stop the proceedings and allow you time to usher him outside. Never rub his nose in his excreta as punishment. *"No!"* or *"Shame!"* appropriately delivered in an admonishing tone is punishment enough.

Paper Breaking

If the puppy you have bought was whelped and weaned in a paper nest then paper-breaking him will be an easy chore. Whatever material he had under his feet in the nest before you brought him home will have a good deal to do with the rapidity with which he is housebroken. He has been conditioned, and will prefer therefore, to excrete on the same kind of material he has felt underfoot and used for this purpose since he was born.

The paper should be placed in a specific area and not moved from there, the best place being a corner of the bathroom, though many people prefer a far corner of the kitchen instead. Watch the puppy for the telltale signs indicating that he is about to relieve himself and, when he begins to squat, take him to the paper immediately and keep him there until he goes. Then praise him highly and tell him what a fine fellow he is. Be consistent and never allow him to go any other place in the house without scolding him and taking him to the paper to show him where he *should* have gone. Sooner than you think (*you hope*) the puppy will be conditioned to run to the place you want him to when nature calls, and use the paper you have supplied for him.

Incidentally, it is best, when you purchase a puppy, to bring him to his new home at the

Color captions

Bouvier des Flandres learns to sit-stay. Jack and Susan Van Vliet, owners, page 17. Airedale Terrier sits close to its owner's side, page 18. Using the "Stay!" command with a Soft-coated Wheaten Terrier. Patricia M. Devlin, owner, page 19. German Shorthaired Pointers learn to pose in a show stance. Herb and Elaine Hollowell, Hidden Hollow Kennels, owners, pages 20-21. Chesapeake Bay Retriever , page 22. Nylon bones can be used to reward good behavior. Norwich Terrier. Mrs. Johan Ostrow, owner, page 23. English Cocker Spaniel. Muriel Clement, Gordon Hill Kennels, owner, page 24.

23

Early Training

beginning of a weekend. Allocate the whole weekend to making the new arrival feel at home and to the job of housebreaking. If you watch him for all the waking hours and catch him each time he has to go, show him where you want him to relieve himself and train him to go there. Though it will be a tedious weekend, it will nevertheless pay big dividends in cutting down the time necessary to housebreak the pup by many hours or even days. Some older puppies can be almost completely housebroken in one weekend of concentrated training.

Avoid hitting a puppy that has relieved itself in the wrong place. Instead, admonish the dog with the word "Shame!" several times.

Box Breaking

If you prefer to train your puppy to evacuate in a box, the material you use in the box is important. If the tyke was born and weaned on sawdust or shavings in the whelping box, supply him with these materials in the shallow box in which you want him to relieve himself. Whatever the material he has experienced underfoot before he came to you should be used in the box. Show him what you want of him in relation to the box, just as in paper breaking, and he will soon be using the box all the time.

Outdoors Breaking

Puppies that have been raised on earth-surfaced runs are the most easily housebroken. Simply take them out to the yard when they are ready and, feeling familiar texture underfoot, they will readily oblige. Other than those who own Toys or very small dogs, the object of an owner is to eventually train a dog to go outside to relieve himself, even though you begin by paper or box breaking your pup. To accomplish this, the paper or box previously soiled by the pup must be moved outside and the puppy brought to it when you figure it is time for him to void. The pup, through his scenting ability, knows what the paper or box has been used for and you will usually have no trouble in urging him to utilize it again for the same purpose.

To reach the point where the puppy no longer needs the paper or box (and will use the ground instead) requires a little time. The paper should be gradually decreased in size until nothing of it remains. The material in the box, after the first few days, should be removed and allowed to be used by the pup without the box. As time passes you must remove a portion of the material each day until only the earth or grass remains. When this long-looked-for time comes your puppy should be fully housebroken. Congratulations!

Incidentally, when you bring the paper from the house to the yard you will probably have to anchor it with stones on each corner or you will awaken some morning to find your housebreaking bait has blown away.

I have stressed using the same material underfoot when housebreaking as the puppy is used to. There is one method of raising puppies that can cause the new owner trouble under certain circumstances. I refer to the use of raised, wire-bottom pens. The idea behind this type of kenneling is to keep puppies from reinfesting themselves with worms or coccidia by allowing excrement to drop through the wire to the ground below. But, since the puppy is accustomed to wire under his feet when he heeds the call of nature, he will seek a similar surface in your home. Therefore, if you have central heating or hot air heat with the grates in the floor, either don't buy that particular pup or change your home before you do buy him.

You can avoid a lot of grief by remembering a few simple rules. Until he is thoroughly clean in the house, confine your pup to a particular room at night and when you leave him alone in the house. Preferably, that room should be one with a tile or linoleum floor that can be easily cleaned. Tie him so that he cannot get beyond the radius of his bed. Few dogs will soil their beds or defecate close to their sleeping quarters. If the pup is still being paper or box broken in the house, whichever of these items he is using should also be within reach.

Feed at regular hours and you will soon learn the interval between the meal and its natural results and get the pup to his toilet area in time.

Give water only after meals until he is housebroken. Puppies are inveterate and constant drinkers if water is easily available, and there is no other way for water to go but out. The result is odd puddles at odd times.

If your pup has extreme difficulty, a trick that can be used to accelerate the pup's housebreaking is the utilization of baby suppositories. Injection of the suppository in the puppy's anus will cause a quick reaction just as it would in a child. The pup brought to the place you wish him to void will do so almost immediately if he has eaten recently and then been treated with the suppository.

Face the problem of housebreaking with aplomb, not with grimness. Laugh off the puddles, piddles, and phews. If you are thorough and determined, with a little cooperation from your pup, you will soon have a housebroken dog and a clean house again.

Collar and Leash Training

I earlier mentioned the wise breeder who adorned his pups with soft collars to which had been tied small pieces of cord. Most puppies, though, have never worn a collar or known the feeling of a leash. Purchase a narrow, soft (but inexpensive) collar and allow the pup to wear it constantly so he will become used to it. I recommend a cheap collar because he will soon outgrow it and you will want something better as a neck adornment for him later on. After he has worn it for two or three days, attach a heavy piece of cord to it—long enough to

Show dogs should be trained at an early age to wear a collar and leash so that they can be handled in the show ring with little difficulty.

reach the ground. After dragging this cord around and tripping over it a time or two, the puppy will be partially leash broken, to the extent anyway that when you snap on the real leash and begin to lead him around he will not fight it if you are gentle.

Never pull a dog around by his leash, and never give the leash to a child and allow the child to pull the dog or pup around.

After the leash has been attached to the collar, call the puppy's name to get his attention. Try to get him to you and walk with you of his own accord. Play out the leash to its full length. Then squat down, call the pup by name, and urge him to *"Come!"* If he should refuse, augment the command by gentle jerks on the leash to bring him to you. Never use a long pull on the leash for any training. Instead always employ quick, short jerks. A tasty tidbit can be used to reward his obedience.

When you have the pup coming to you from the length of the leash, get a much lighter rope, 15 to 20 feet long, attach it to his collar, and repeat the same exercises you used with the leash.

If your pup is running free and you call to him to *"Come!"* but he doesn't heed your command, do *not* chase him—he will only run away and dodge your attempts to catch him and you will lose control, over yourself as well as over the pup, and many hours of training will have been wasted. Be calm; attract his

Early Training

attention by calling his name and, when he looks in your direction, turn and run *away* from him, looking back meanwhile and calling him to come. In most instances he will quickly run after you. Don't grab him when he reaches you. Instead squat or sit down on the ground and laugh and pet him when he comes up. Even if it takes a great deal of time and much exasperation to get him to come to you, never scold him once he has, but praise him instead. If you scold him he will not know that his punishment is for *not coming*. He will associate the act of punishment with his immediate deed and will think that he is being punished for *coming* to you.

In the early stages of leash training with young puppies, be content with merely teaching the

Trainers of hunting dogs will often discharge a gun when their puppies are preoccupied with eating so that they learn to disregard loud noises such as gunshot sounds.

pup to move freely on the leash while only occasionally tangling it around your legs. When he is walking easily next to you, begin using the command *"Heel!"* to familiarize him with it. But don't attempt to make the pup rigidly *"Heel!"* until he is older. More comprehensive lessons in teaching to *"Heel!"* will be presented in a later chapter.

Feeding as Part of Training

Food plays a great part in your dog's training. We have seen how very early feeding makes him familiar with his call name and teaches him that there is a reward awaiting him when he

29

Early Training

responds. The tidbit utilized in training as a reward is also a part of the overall feeding of the puppy to exact obedience. Training the dog to accept loud noises so that he will not be gun or thunder shy can also be accomplished during the feeding period. Trainers of hunting dogs begin teaching their future hopefuls to disregard gunshot sounds during the time they are being fed. Hungry puppies are so intensely absorbed in the process of gulping down as much food as possible in as little time as possible, particularly when fed together with their littermates, that they are prone to disregard anything, including noise, that will turn them from their purpose.

The hunting dog trainer takes advantage of this absorption of the puppy in his competitive feeding by discharging a gun a short distance from where the pups are eating. The report is probably not even noticed by the food-frantic pups, but is absorbed by their subconscious minds. The trainer gradually moves closer during subsequent feeding times until he can stand immediately above the youngsters and discharge the gun without disturbing them. They have been conditioned to the sound and know, by the time they become completely aware of it, that it holds no terrors for them.

It is very much worthwhile to train all puppies to be unafraid of sharp sounds and loud noises. You need not use a gun to accomplish this design. Simply take the top of a large metal can (such as a garbage can) and, when the pups are completely absorbed in their food, drop it on the floor at a short distance from where they are feeding. Gradually move closer until you can drop the top immediately behind the pups without the racket bothering them in the least. If one or two of the pups stop eating and are disturbed by the sound, soothe them and make less noise until you see that they have built up a tolerance to the sound. Storms, thunder, backfiring from autos, gunfire, and other sudden loud noises will find the dogs steady and fearless.

Even your own periods of

Early Training

Never feed your dog (or other pets) from the table while you are eating your meals; always offer your pets their own feeding dishes.

feeding, the human mealtimes, can be used to advantage in helping to train your dog. Do not *ever* feed your dog tidbits from the table while you are eating, or he will become a mealtime pest, continually begging for food and drooling unbecomingly at the thought of attaining his desire.

Select a specific spot or area for your dog during your mealtime, and make him lie down and stay there without pestering you or anyone else at the table. A corner of the dining room is a desirable place for him to lie and wait until you are finished.

The Goals of Training

The basis of all this early training is the desire to fit your puppy into your household and make him a well behaved member of the family. The basis of all training, with dogs as it is with children, is to make them better citizens when they reach maturity by conditioning them to learning patterns of behavior and, through teaching, to acquire knowledge. With this early training as a foundation, your puppy can go on to more complicated training and you, as his owner, are the proper person to give him that training.

Many dog owners are afraid to attempt anything that smacks of advanced training. If you have successfully taught your puppy the elements of early training, including that bugaboo of the neophyte owner, housebreaking, then an attitude of apprehension toward future training is ridiculous. You have already established control and have conditioned your puppy to learn and obey your commands. The most difficult, basic part is over.

Early Training

Future training will be but building on the foundation you have already laid.

Later, when you are engaged in advanced training, you will probably want to join a training group, one of which you will find operating in, or close to, your neighborhood. To work in the company of other people and other dogs will prove stimulating for both you and your pupil. But remember that the basis of this schooling is exactly the same as you will learn from this book—to teach you to train your dog.

Keep calm; don't shout commands, or your puppy may eventually come to think that they are reprimands. Use your voice to create word sounds that have meaning to your puppy, and never lose control of yourself. If you do, you will lose the control you must have over your pupil, that control which is the most important part of training, the control that is the element you must use to condition your dog in the behavior patterns that will make him a well trained, well liked, and admired canine citizen.

All Dogs Need to Chew

Puppies and young dogs need something with resistance to chew on while their teeth and jaws are developing—for cutting the puppy teeth, to induce growth of the permanent teeth under the puppy teeth, to assist in getting rid of the puppy teeth at the proper time, to help the permanent teeth through the gums, to assure normal jaw development and to settle the permanent teeth solidly in the jaws.

The adult dog's desire to chew stems from the instinct for tooth cleaning, gum massage and jaw exercise—plus the need for an outlet for periodic doggie tensions.

This is why dogs, especially puppies and young dogs, will often destroy property worth hundreds of dollars, when their chewing instinct is not diverted from their owner's possessions, particularly during the widely varying critical period for young dogs.

Saving your possessions from destruction, assuring proper

Early Training

development of teeth and jaws, providing for 'interim' tooth cleaning and gum massage, and channeling doggie tensions into a non-destructive outlet are,

Chewing helps keep the dog's teeth and gums in good condition. Be sure to give your pet something safe to chew on and divert its attention from those objects that are off limits.

therefore, all dependent upon the dog having something suitable for chewing readily available when his instinct tells him to chew. If your purposes, and those of your dog, are to be accomplished, what you provide for chewing must be desirable from the doggie viewpoint, have the necessary functional qualities, and above all, be safe for your dog.

It is very important that dogs not be permitted to chew on anything they can break, or indigestible things from which they can bite sizeable chunks. Sharp pieces, from such as a bone which can be broken by a dog, may pierce the intestine wall and kill. Indigestible things which can be bitten off in chunks, such as toys made of rubber compound or plastic, may cause an intestinal stoppage, if not regurgitated—to bring painful death, unless surgery is promptly performed.

An old leather shoe is another popular answer to the chewing need—but be very sure that the rubber heel, all nails, and other metal parts such as lace grommets, metal arches, etc., have been removed. Be especially careful to get all of the nails. A chunk of rubber heel can cause an intestinal stoppage. If it has a nail in it, the intestine wall may be pierced or torn. Then there is, of course, always the hazard that your dog may fail to differentiate between his shoe and yours, and eat up a good pair while you're not looking.

Early Training

Dried rawhide products of various types, shapes, sizes and prices are available on the market and have become quite popular. However, they don't serve the primary chewing functions very well; they are a bit messy when wet from mouthing, and most dogs chew them up rather rapidly—but they have been considered safe for dogs until recently. Now, more and more incidents of death, and near death, by strangulation have been reported to be the result of partially swallowed chunks of rawhide swelling in the throat. More recently, some veterinarians have been attributing cases of acute constipation to large pieces of incompletely digested rawhide in the intestine.

Advantages of Nylon Bones

The nylon bones, especially those with natural meat and bone fractions added, are probably the most complete, safe and economical answer to the chewing need. Dogs cannot break them or bite off sizeable chunks; hence, they are completely safe—and being longer lasting than other things offered for the purpose, they are economical.

Hard chewing raises little bristle-like projections on the surface of the nylon bones—to provide effective interim tooth cleaning and vigorous gum massage, much in the same way your tooth brush does it for you. The little projections are raked off and swallowed in the form of thin shavings—but the chemistry of the nylon is such that they break down in the stomach fluids and pass through without effect.

Nylabones are especially recommended as chewing aids since they are safe (they won't splinter or chip) and economical.

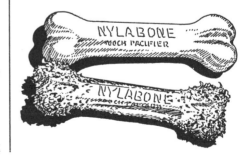

34

Early Training

The toughness of the nylon provides the strong chewing resistance needed for important jaw exercise and effective help for the teething functions—but there is no tooth wear because nylon is non-abrasive. Being inert, nylon does not support the growth of microorganisms—and it can be washed in soap and water, or it can be sterilized by boiling or in an autoclave.

Nylabone® is highly recommended by veterinarians as a safe, healthy nylon bone that can't splinter or chip. Instead, Nylabone is frizzled by the dog's chewing action, creating a toothbrush-like surface that cleanses the teeth and massages the gums. Nylabone® and Nylaball® , the only chew

Prevent your puppies from chewing on various soft goods (old clothing and linens, for example); loose threads or small torn pieces could be swallowed.

products made of flavor-impregnated solid nylon, are available in your local pet shop.

Nothing, however, substitutes for periodic professional attention to your dog's teeth and gums, not any more than your toothbrush can do that for you. Have your dog's teeth cleaned by your veterinarian at least once a year; twice a year is better—and he will be healthier, happier and far more pleasant to live with.

Tricks of Training

Puppies learn from the harsh tone of your voice that you are displeased with their bad behavior.

There generally comes a time in the training of your young puppy, or even the older dog, when a method can be utilized that tricks the animal into the wanted behavior. This type of training is called the *negative* approach and is exactly opposite to the more widely and generally used *postive* approach. It is, in the truest sense, a form of trickery and, being disassociated from *positive* training, is also divorced from the basic control so necessary in all direct training.

These tricks are used when positive methods have failed and you feel that any drastic punishment for the pupil's failure might harm, rather than help, your training program. The basic idea behind this training trickery is to make the dog think that he is punishing himself, so the result of his disobedience must become an unforgettable experience. In the pup's mind you, his master and trainer, will have had no association with the catastrophe.

Stealing Food from the Table

This is an act most puppies can't resist. Their exploding rate of growth pushing them to almost constant hunger, human food on the table is a delicacy they can't fight. This is particularly true of dogs that have been fed small tidbits from the table by some member of the family, one of the easiest ways to spoil a dog. Most puppies who have been scolded harshly for stealing from the table are smart enough not to attempt their crime until you are out of the room and the coast is clear. Then they will quickly and quietly sneak up to the table, delicately reach for and gobble down any food within reach, especially meat.

If your puppy, or dog, has become an inveterate thief and no amount of scolding can keep him from his shamefaced robbery when the opportunity offers, then you must turn to the negative or tricky way of correcting this misdemeanor. Arrange the table as you always do when he attempts to steal from it. Then take a tempting piece of meat, tie a string to it and to the other end of the string attach some tin cans (*empty*), bells, and whatever else you can think of that will make a racket when disturbed. Now place the piece of meat on the edge of the table. Do *not* allow the dog to watch you while you prepare his surprise. You must in no way be implicated in what is about to happen.

When all is ready leave the room as you have on previous occasions when the pup has ravished the table during your absence. When you are out of the room and the puppy stealthily approaches the table and grabs the meat, he will inadvertently pull the assortment of noisemakers attached to the other end of the string down from the table and, if he attempts to run from this frightening cacophony, it will follow him as long as he retains the stolen piece of meat in his mouth. The shock this will cause him is about the same as a sneak thief would feel who has stealthily and silently entered a home to steal and, upon opening the bureau drawer, is suddenly assailed by the earsplitting din of a brass band's close-up rendition of a Sousa march.

Careful, intense silence is the sneak-thief's cover, and once that quiet is shattered he is left naked and exposed. The sneak-thief puppy feels this same way with the din that he has caused echoing in his ears and pointing him out as the culprit.

Jumping on Furniture

The same kind of approach is used for the pup who persists, even in the face of punishment, upon jumping up and sleeping on the living room furniture. After repeated punishment he will generally only do this when you are out of the room, or the house, and will jump down as soon as he hears you returning. Telltale hair on the cushions of sofa or easy-chair is the only clue to his disobedience. To break the sly tyke of this habit we again use the negative approach and resort to trickery to make him

Your dog must learn not to jump up on the furniture, if this is what you desire.

"NO!"

think that he is punishing himself and that you have had nothing to do with it at all. Purchase several small mouse traps, set them and deposit them on the sofa or chair which the pup seems to favor. Then gently cover the traps with a piece of brown wrapping paper or several sheets of newspaper. Leave the room and await developments. Again let me caution you to set your trap in secret so that the victim is completely unaware that you have had a hand in his eventual consternation.

If you are close by when the pup nonchalantly leaps up to take his ease on your furniture you will hear the snapping of the smothered traps and the frantic yelp of the pup followed by his immediate departure from the vicinity. The dog can't be hurt—only startled and completely disconcerted by the snapping of the traps and the movement that accompanies this phenomena under the protective paper.

If your pup or dog is an unwelcome occupier of your bed when you aren't looking, and

Some owners train their dogs to sit on a particular piece of furniture but discourage the animals from others.

scolding has had no effect, the identical method used above will have the same curative result. Of course one way of avoiding all difficulty of this sort is to confine your dog to a specific area when you leave the house or are out of the room or occupied elsewhere. This area would not allow him to be near bedroom or living room and so temptation would be removed. But to my mind it is better to allow the dog, assuming he is fully housebroken, the run of the house and to face and correct any training problems that follow in the wake of this freedom.

Jumping up on People

Dogs of boisterous temperament have a tendency to constantly jump up on their master, mistress, the people of the household and all visiting friends. In this way they exhibit their joy of life and love of you. But this happy greeting can be the means of your losing innumerable and valuable friends when your mud-footed dog jumps up on some natty visitor who is wearing a new suit or dress. Such behavior can even exasperate you, the animal's loving owner.

There are positive training methods that can be employed to break this habit that will be explained later. But now I will explain another trick to use if the *"No!"* command alone does not break him of this habit. When he jumps up grinning and pawing, grab his front feet and retain your hold, meanwhile greeting him with good-humored tolerance. The pup finds himself in an uncomfortable position standing on his hind legs alone, a position not quite suitable or natural for one of the canine species. He will soon tire of standing in such a way and begin to pull and tug to release his front paws from your hands and return to a normal position with all four paws on terra firma. Retain your hold in the face of this gradually more frantic struggle until he has become heartily sick of his position and the whole idea. A few such lessons and he will refrain from committing an act that brings such discomfort in its wake.

Success in training can vary greatly among the different breeds of dog.

You will probably be able to think of other little tricks that you can improvise to outsmart your dog in some area of conduct. But remember that these tricks are only short-cut ways of rectifying nuisance habits, and do nothing to establish the control and *"rapport"* which must exist between trainer and dog in the important area of positive training.

More Tricks of Training

I have seen trainers use a strange mode of punishment which seems to have worked with some puppies. A rolled up piece of paper is used, preferably brown wrapping paper, not newspaper. When the puppy chews upon a forbidden object, his master's shoe let us say, the trainer, with the puppy kept close so that he will not miss what happens, uses the rolled paper to strike and punish the *shoe*, not the puppy. Some pups react by never again touching the punished object or any others like it. But I have also seen the opposite occur and have had puppies attack and attempt to aid their master in his punishment of the naughty object.

It is essential that puppies as well as grown dogs be given their freedom and allowed to run off leash often. Many dogs, kept confined to the leash, act like wild idiots when set free. Sometimes such animals run so far and fast that they are quickly out of sight and seem deaf to the frantic calls of their owners. One way to cure this habit is, of course, to give them more freedom. But there is a way to condition your dog to stay closer to you when walking or running off leash. This, too, is a trick, but one that is fun for both you and your dog. Simply hide when he begins to get too far away, then call or whistle him to you. Upon looking back he won't see you and will come searching until he finds you. If he seems to be unable to find you, give your position away by some movement or slight noise. It is a game he will enjoy, but in the playing of it he will learn to constantly look back to make sure you are in sight and he will always stay fairly close so that he can return immediately to enjoy your game of hide-and-go-seek.

By holding a tidbit high over your dog's head so that he must strain to peer up at it, and inadvertently sits to be more comfortable, is a method sometimes employed by trainers to make a dog sit. The word *"Sit!"* is spoken when the dog lowers his hindquarters to the ground for comfort.

Dog psychologists have long used negative methods of conditioning animal reflexes to get specific training results. The bell and meal test is well known. Dogs, conditioned to be fed at certain hours, were alerted to the feeding time by the ringing of a bell. Eventually just the ringing of the bell would bring saliva to the dog's mouth even though food was not forthcoming.

Using small metal clickers is another approach psychologists have used in conditioning behavior patterns of dogs. When the dog naturally indulges in a specific action, such as turning toward a corner of the room, the psychologist clicks the little tin instrument. Soon he has

Tricks of Training

The command "Sit!" is part of basic dog training.

conditioned the dog to turn toward that specific corner of the room every time the clicker sounds.

I have used this type of conditioning myself in training. It takes tremendous concentration, complete absorption in the task at hand, and time without interruption spent with the pupil. I taught a nine months old bitch to sit and lie down by staying with her constantly for three days. Every time she would normally sit I would utter the command, *"Sit!"*

Every time she would naturally lie down I said, *"Lie down!"* I did not touch her or ever force her to obey these commands, I simply stayed with her constantly as a completely absorbed observer and each time she performed, of her own accord, either of the desired actions I gave the proper command as she executed them. She was soon conditioned to obey these commands immediately without having been forced into the proper positions by positive training. Granted it was a tedious and time-consuming task, but it nevertheless proved to my own satisfaction that it could be done with gratifying results.

Remember that when you use these tricks to condition your dog to behave the way you want him to, you are not actually training him; you are only tricking him to perform certain acts that will mold his conduct, and this method of negative training is limited in scope. I could go on, telling you of other similar means of training such as those used by hunters, where a reward of meat and punishment through

Tricks of Training

electric shock is used in negative training. Electrical devices can be constructed to fit the dog's collar and used to shock him when he disobeys in training. Electric prods, such as cattlemen use, are also utilized by some trainers. I am personally against all training methods, negative or positive, that are based on cruel punishment. Shocking or actually hurting a dog is not necessary in basic training. Such methods are the devices of sadists, or calloused individuals who should not own dogs.

If you own a dog that you can't control or train, do not beat him or use cruel methods in your attempt to train him. Take him instead to a qualified dog trainer, explain your problem to him, and allow him to train your dog for you. It is the business of such experts to deal with problem dogs or to train dogs for specialized tasks.

Car Training

To train your pup to ride with aplomb in the family car is merely a matter of repetition. Make the first few rides very short, increasing the distance as he gains in his ability to endure the movement of the car without upset. Always make sure that he enters the car for these lessons with an empty stomach. Dogs love to accompany their masters, or any member of the family, when they go for a drive.

Of course there is another kind of car training and that is breaking your dog from chasing cars if he has acquired that nasty and dangerous habit. Attach to his collar a heavy cord to which a piece of broomstick is horizontally hung, just low enough to bounce sharply against his legs if he starts running, is a negative method of training. If the ordinary *"No!"* or *"Shame!"* or the broomstick doesn't stop him from continuing this practice, then a harsher method must be used. This must be accomplished with the assistance of someone in a car which we assume he will chase. The person in the car must be supplied with a water pistol filled with water, and while the car is in motion and the dog chases it, he must squirt the dog full in the face with the water. If this method still proves fruitless, a weak solution of ammonia should be used in the water pistol instead of plain water. This might seem like a drastic means of combating such behavior, but you must remember that the end result of car chasing is either the death of your dog under the wheels of some speeding vehicle, or the wreck of a chased car with human injury and possible loss of life as an aftermath.

Through practice, your dog can learn to accompany you on car trips. Make certain, however, that your pet has an empty stomach to avoid getting car sick.

Serious Training Begins

What you have learned about training in this book up to now has been preliminary training for the young puppy, with the exception of a very few lessons such as car chasing, etc. Between the ages of two and six months your puppy should have absorbed all the teaching that has gone before. Now we approach the time of serious training.

Setting up a Schedule

If possible, it is best to arrange two training sessions a day. Begin with ten-minute sessions if you can manage two a day. If you only have time for one training session, limit the time to no more than half an hour. Observe your dog during the training period and you will be able to tell when he begins to become bored with the whole thing. That is the time to quit. As you and your pupil advance in your schooling, the time limit can be extended.

The training commands you are about to teach your dog are the most important in relation to fashioning your pet into a fine and gentlemanly companion. The lessons he will learn are: to sit, to heel, to lie down, to come when called, to stand upon command, and to stay when told in the sit, down, and stand positions. He will learn a few other commands, too, if you wish to teach them to him, but those just mentioned are the commands of basic schooling.

Before we begin, let us be sure that we are in an area where there will be no activity that will distract the dog from concentration on his work. Review in your mind all that you have learned so far about control and all the other elements of training in relation to you and your dog. Check your equipment and be sure that the choke-chain collar is being correctly worn (so that it tightens from above and not below your dog's neck) and that the leash is gathered easily in your right hand. You will also use your left hand on the leash, but the bulk of the leash must be gathered and held in your right hand. Remember always to work your dog from your left side.

Serious Training Begins

And do *not* allow your pupil to consider this as play. He must be taught that these periods of training are serious and are work, and that following them he will be allowed to play to his heart's content.

Training to "Sit!"

You have probably given your puppy some schooling in this exercise already. But now he must be taught how to sit exactly

Praise your dog with a "Good boy!" or "Good girl!" whenever the animal promptly assumes the correction position on the command "Sit!".

and immediately when given the command, and to do it on leash at your side.

Maneuver the dog to your left side and, hold the leash in your right hand to allow your left hand to be free and to give you about a foot of slack in the leash from the dog's neck to your right hand. Get your dog's quick attention by speaking his name, immediately followed by the command *"Sit!"* Issue the command firmly and clearly in your best training voice. As you do, pull upward on the leash until the collar begins to tighten and, with your free left hand, reach back, and place your palm on his croup or rump, your fingers facing toward his tail. Now press downward firmly with your left hand to force his hind legs to fold and his hind end to collapse into a sitting position. While you do this be sure that you keep the leash held in your right hand fairly taut so that you hold his head and the front part of the dog up.

When your pupil is in the correct position, give praise with a *"Good boy!"* or *"Good girl!"* as

Serious Training Begins

the case may be. Incidentally, throughout this book I have assumed that the pupil is masculine. Believe me, I have nothing against the feminine gender, animal, mineral, vegetable, or what-have-you. On the contrary, under most circumstances I rather favor the feminine. In this instance, though, I simply find it easier to use the masculine gender when referring to the pupil.

When you have your pupil sitting nicely at your side, relax the tautness of the leash as you praise him, but attempt to keep him sitting. To do this you must be quiet, not boisterous in your praise. Now, with a quick, gentle tug on the leash, move forward a step to bring your dog standing and at your side. Repeat the lesson again, being careful not to tighten the leash too sharply as you reach down and push the dog's hindquarters down. Straighten your body and keep the dog sitting for a few seconds at your side before you step forward to repeat it again.

Should your dog quit sitting and stand of his own accord,

then it is not necessary to step forward before repeating the command. But you must not allow him to bounce back up to his feet immediately. When you feel the dog's rump begin to yield under your hand as you press down and give the *"Sit!"* command, use less pressure to make him sit, until the mere touch of a finger on his croup gets the desired result. Soon, then, you will not have to touch him at all, just speak the command and he will sit quietly at your side.

If your dog will not hold the sit position for more than a second or two before he breaks, scold him with a *"No!"* and make him take the position again. Should he lie down when told to sit, don't attempt to pull him up by the leash; lift him from in front until he is in the *"Sit!"* position. Correct his position by placing your hand on his rump either to the right or the left side when you push down, which ever side will correct his posture if he sits crookedly.

The sit is the easiest of all the

Serious Training Begins

This dog has learned various obedience commands.

exercises, which is why I recommend that it be taught first. But, being the first lesson, it must be learned perfectly. Therefore do not settle for less than perfection from your pupil. Do not tolerate any degree of sloppiness. Your dog must sit promptly and squarely at your side when given the *"Sit!"* command. Though at the beginning it is permissible to use the command several times as you push down on his rump to make him obey, after he has learned what you want of him give the command just once, using his name first, *"Jerry, sit!"*

This first lesson, to sit properly, will set the tone for all the schooling to come. Both you

and your dog will learn a great deal before you move on to the next lesson. It is up to you to see that your dog learns to be a perfectionist in his execution of this simple command.

In an earlier section I told you how I tricked a bitch into obeying the *"sit"* and *"down"* commands by speaking the proper order each time she, of her own accord, began to sit or lie down. Such negative conditioning can be indulged in when the puppy is very young, but I do not recommend that it be used in the direct and positive training that you have now begun. I was conducting an experiment with an older bitch when I used this form of approach, a very tedious experiment I might add, and not one to be used after positive-conditioning schooling has been successfully started.

The importance of the *"Sit!"* command, and its exact execution, will become obvious later. In the training to come you will find that most of the new lessons will begin from the sit position.

Training to "Heel"

The *"sit"* position has trained your dog to sit nicely at your side where he is ready to begin to learn how to *"heel."* He need not be perfect in the *"sit"* before you begin this new lesson. As a matter of fact, after the pupil is doing fairly well in obeying the *"sit"* command and you sense that he is becoming restless, it is then time to switch to the new lesson of *"heeling."*

Stand straight with the dog in a good sit position at your side. The leash should be gathered in your right hand with the left hand grasping the leash so that it hangs from the dog's collar with about two feet of slack. Your left leg should be close to the dog's shoulder, touching it if possible. Now you step briskly forward, with your left foot first, using a definite, long stride. As you do this you jerk quickly on the leash with your left hand and give the command, *"Brucie, heel!"* Speak his name a split second before you stride forward to get his quick attention, and follow it with the command and the leash tug. His name prepares him for action and your movement forward and jerk on the leash is the action with which he will couple the command.

Repeat the command *"Heel!"* (now without the animal's call name) every few steps once you get him moving. At first he will probably run ahead, drag behind, or lurch to the side. Whatever he may do can be controlled by short jerks on the leash with your left hand once you get him moving. Always be sure that there is slack in the leash, otherwise you will not be able to jerk it so that the chain choke collar tightens quickly and is released again, which is the measure of your control over the pupil.

Once you have the dog moving fairly well in the heel position in a straight line, make a sharp right turn, alerting the animal with a tug on the leash and the command *"Heel!"* Walk straight forward again for forty or fifty steps, or to a given mark, and repeat the right turn using the same means of conveying your wants to the pupil as you did before. After you have completed a square in this manner, make a

49

complete right about turn, speaking the *"Heel!"* command supplemented by a tug on the leash, or several tugs if necessary to get him around.

Continue a few more right-about turns with the appropriate command and leash jerks, and then come to a halt and command your pupil to sit. If he seems confused and doesn't sit immediately, reach down with your left hand and touch or put slight pressure upon his croup to remind him of what he must do.

Combine these two commands, *"Heel"* and *"Sit,"* until your dog automatically comes to a sit position at your side when you come to a halt. In other words, he will sit without command when you have him at heel and come to a complete halt.

Once he has assimilated the heeling lesson and walks nicely at your side close to your knee, there is no need to keep repeating the *"Heel!"* command unless you are about to make a turn. Now, since he no longer needs the small tugs or leash jerks for signals to keep at heel, your left hand will be free to give him a visual as well as an oral signal and command to heel. This is done by gently slapping the side of your thigh as you give the signal to *"Heel!"* Soon your dog will learn to watch for the visual "Heel!" signal and it will no longer be necessary for you to augment it with the oral command. On turns the slap of your hand against your leg will gain his alert attention as did your spoken *"Heel!"* before.

The "Halt" Signal

When you train the dog to "Heel!" you must, necessarily, come eventually to a stop. To keep your animal from continuing his forward movement when you come to a stop, you must employ the signal "Halt!" A step or two before you come to a stop and utter the "Halt!" command, tighten up on the leash to prepare your pupil for what is to come. Soon he will know that this tightening of the leash is a signal and he will be alert to the command *"Halt!"* If he continues walking when you

Training to "Heel"

stop, don't pull him back with a long, forceful pull on the leash. Use instead the short jerks, slap your thigh and call him to *"Heel!"* Continue the exercise until he knows and reacts faithfully to the command *"Halt!"*

This hunting dog has gone through the rigors of obedience training so that on hunting expeditions it will be the perfect companion.

During the lessons in heeling, no matter what your dog does, short of throwing himself to the ground and lying on his back, you must continue walking at a steady gait. If he goes wide at the turns, bring him to you with short jerks on the leash, but do not stop your steady forward stride. When he closes up nicely on the turns, reward him with a *"Good boy!"* but don't slow down or quit your precise forward walking. Of course, your pace must be matched to the size of your pupil. A brisk pace for a German Shepherd or Labrador would keep a Peke or Boston at an impossible run. Some breeds are capable of moving faster than others, so accommodate your pace to that of the breed your pupil represents.

Work your dog in the *"Sit"* and *"Heeling"* exercises for at least three training sessions, or three training days if his training is scheduled for one session daily.

When you begin teaching your dog to left turn while heeling, step to the left with your left leg, the leg closest to the dog. This almost automatically turns him to the left. With smaller dogs you can step in front of and turn them by jerks on the leash. Mix up your turns during the lessons to keep your pupil attentive and to condition him always to be alert while heeling so that he will not miss a turn.

Often, after your dog has

Training to "Heel"

learned to *"Heel!"* properly and well, he will begin to move a bit ahead of you and in this way miss turns. Small dogs can usually be corrected by jerks on the leash to bring them back to the proper position. This will sometimes work with larger dogs, too. But if it doesn't, we must try another way to keep him from surging too far forward while at heel. Allow the slack of the leash, that you have up to now held gathered in your hand, to fall loose, over your hand. The long training leash should allow three to four feet of slack to hang from your right hand, with the leash's looped handle at the end. Now begin to whirl this slack around in a circle in front of you as you move your dog forward in the *"Heel!"* position. As soon as he begins to surge too far in front, the whirling end of the leash will hit his nose and he will draw back from it. Continue this treatment until the dog stays properly at your side when heeling.

This way of correction is, of course, a trick, not positive teaching. The dog does not associate his punishment with either you or the leash. He feels that he has brought it upon himself by moving into the path of the whirling leash.

Let us suppose that your animal genius has quickly learned how to sit and heel and does both with a nice flourish. It is time then to introduce you, your pupil, and your little smile of triumph to our next set of exercises.

After learning to sit and to heel, your dog can be trained to sit-stay.

Training to "Sit-Stay"

We have taught your dog a hand signal for heeling and it is now time to teach him to *"Stay"* while at the *"Sit"* position and introduce him to a hand signal to supplement the oral command in this exercise. We will also teach him to obey a hand signal for the "Sit" alone, and from a position in front of the dog.

"Sit-stay!"

Let us begin with the *"Sit-stay!"* because after learning the *"Sit"* and *"Heel"* exercises he will be in the natural position to be taught this new lesson.

Begin with your dog in the now familiar sit position at heel on your left side. The leash is gathered as usual in your right hand. Now reach down with your free left hand with the palm flat and toward the dog and put the flat of your palm, fingers pointing toward the ground, in front of his nose. Speak the command, *"Sit-stay!"* As you give the command, step out and away from the pupil with your *right* leg.

Remember that when we taught our student to heel we always led with our *left* foot forward. That was to remove the close support of that leg from beside the dog so that he knew that you were moving away and would begin to follow. This time, when teaching him the *"Sit-stay,"* we want him to remain where he is; so we step out first with the other leg, the right one.

As you step forward, pass the leash from your right to your left hand and, from your long stride away, turn to face the dog. Hold the leash high and rather taut to control him, repeating as you face him *"Sit-stay!"* Your repeat of the command and the tightening of the leash, held at arm's length over the dog, is designed to keep the animal from following you.

If he stays in the sit position upon command when you stand in front of him, reverse everything you have just done and go back to his side again. Go through the whole procedure again and continue to do so until he sits firmly at the command

Training to "Sit-Stay"

and when you leave his side and evidently knows what you want him to do. Now you can vary the procedure by taking a step to the left, a step to the right, when you face him, and finally walk completely around him, always ending up at his side and always beginning with the first step forward and the turn to face him. Keep repeating the command, *"Stay!"* to hold him in the proper position, using it as often as necessary. If he indicates that he is about to rise and come to you, utter the command sharply.

The leash now held in your left hand, to which you passed it when you stepped forward away from the dog, leaves your right hand free. Your right hand should be held out toward the pupil with the palm up, fingers pointing upward, in the *"Stay!"* sign. Though the fingers pointed downward when you first gave the signal in front of the animal's nose as you stepped away from him, the flattened palm turned toward him is, to the dog, the visual signal of the *"Stay!"* command whether the fingers point up or down.

Second Step of "Sit-Stay!"

When the pupil will remain in the *"Sit-stay!"* for ten or fifteen seconds as you engage in taking your one stride away in several directions while holding the leash at arm's length above him to check his movement, you may begin the second step of this exercise.

Exchange the leash for a long, thin (but strong) nylon cord about thirty feet long. Go through the same *"Sit-stay!"* routine as you did when the dog was wearing a leash instead of the rope which now replaces it. But this time do not attempt to hold the rope up and over the dog's head to restrain him as you did before. Instead, allow the rope to hang loose. When the exercise is finished to your satisfaction, praise your pupil lavishly.

Again you must repeat the whole routine from the beginning. However, as you step away don't just take one step; take two. Watch the dog closely and be ready to check any movement toward you with a

Training to "Sit-Stay"

sharp, *"Sit-stay!"* Move around him in a circle and widen the circle as you progress, until you have played out half the rope and can circle him at a distance of about fifteen feet. Return to him and your proper position next to him, praise him and release him. If he will *"Sit-stay!"* for a full minute while you circle him and return, he has done well.

If your dog simply will not *"Sit-stay!"* as you step forward, begin the exercise by stepping to the side away from him. This

When you can walk in a circle around your dog (about fifteen feet away from it) and it remains in the sit-stay position, then the dog has learned the command well.

often corrects any tendency he may have to stand and follow you.

Most trainers use the palm-toward-the-dog signal for the *"Sit-stay,"* as I have indicated before. It is fine to use as you leave your dog's side, but it has been my experience that it is an awkward gesture once you face your dog. I personally prefer to use a raised, rather admonishing forefinger of the right hand as the "Sit-stay!" sign once I have left the dog's side and stepped in front of him.

Training to "Down!"

There are several ways to accomplish this exercise depending upon the individual dog, his size, and temperament. If your dog is small enough, the easiest method is to begin in the usual manner with your dog at the *"Sit!"* position at your left side. With the leash gathered in your right hand, reach down with your left, leaning over the dog, and with the flat of your palm press down on his

Training to "Sit-Stay"

shoulders (withers) until you force him to lie down, accompanying the downward push with the vocal command, *"Prince, Down!"* Repeat the word *"Down!"* over and over again to keep him in the down position once you have forced him into it.

If your dog is a member of one of the larger breeds, and he resists your downward push to the extent where it becomes almost impossible to accomplish your objective, then you must approach this exercise from a different angle.

Begin with the *"Sit-stay!"* and when you are facing the pupil reach forward as you give the command, grasp the dog's front legs just above the feet and pull the feet toward you. This action will cause the animal's body to drop down to the ground and he will be in the *"Down!"* position. As soon as he has inadvertently assumed this posture, put the flat of your palm on his shoulders and press downward to hold him there, meanwhile repeating the command over and over again.

Should your dog be stubborn and adamant in his refusal to

"Down!" and the above approaches have failed, then we must resort to yet another method. Begin again as you have before with the dog at *"Sit-stay!"* with you, the trainer, facing your dog. Hold the leash in your left hand with enough slack in it so that it loops a few inches above the ground. Now put your left foot over the leash so that the lowest section is under your instep. Speak the command *"Down!"* and simultaneously pull up on the leash and press down with your foot to the ground. This action will tighten the choke chain and put a downward pressure on the dog forcing him into the desired position.

Color captions
Chesapeake Bay Retriever at home in the water, page 57. Labrador Retrievers are fine hunting companions, page 58. The German Shepherd breed is especially suited to guard work, page 59. This Chesapeake Bay Retriever dives into the water upon command, pages 60-61. Standard Schnauzer learning to heel. Elizabeth G. Hanrahan, owner, page 62. The Newfoundland, a sturdy working dog, can be easily trained as a household guardian. Here a Newfoundland enjoys a backyard romp. Phil and Mary Lauer, Evangeline Kennels, owners, page 63. Airedale learning to shake hands, page 64.

Training to "Come!"

In an earlier chapter I stressed the fact that you must never scold or punish your dog when he has come to you regardless of the provocation. If you have not followed this advice, or if you have forgotten it, you will pay for your negligence now in the *"Come when called"* exercise.

Exact obedience to this command is absolutely essential, for it can save your dog's life and keep you from embarrassment. There is nothing more exasperating than attempting to catch a loose dog that won't come to you. Your pupil has learned the rudiments of the *"Come!"* command, as he has several of the other directives, when he was much younger. But now it is time to condition him to obey faithfully, absolutely, and with alacrity the moment the command is uttered.

To begin this exercise (known in obedience parlance as the *"recall"*), we bring the pupil to the *"sit"* position at our side, give him the command and the hand signal to *"Sit-stay!"* and walk away in front of him to the limiting length of the loosely held leash in your right hand. Command him to *"Spot, Come!"* in a crisp voice and simultaneously jerk on the leash to direct him toward you. Guide him to a position directly in front of you with quick leash tugs and the crisply spoken command. When he has accomplished your desire, pet and praise him lavishly.

Remember that you have given him a direct order, the *"Stay!"* which he is now being asked to break or disregard and, if you have succeeded in training him truly and well, it will be difficult for him to respond without reluctance. Because the pupil is loathe to disobey the *"Stay!"* command, you must do whatever you can to coax him to obey the recall. Your position as you give the command will help. Kneel, squat, or lean far over toward him, positions that have a beguiling effect upon the dog, acting as a compulsion to movement toward you. Slap your knee gently as a hand signal which is also an aid in compelling him to come to you.

Do *not* give him the *"Sit"*

command when he has arrived at a position directly before you. The accomplishment of the *"Come!"* is enough to warrant your unmitigated praise. If he *should* sit in front of you in completing the *"Come!"* exercise, it is an added bonus.

Use of the Long Line

Once the pupil understands the *"Come!"* command and executes it with commendable speed on leash, the next step is to train him to come from a greater distance through the use of the long rope. Remove the leash and attach the nylon (or rope) line to his collar. Starting with the *"Sit!"* position, use the line exactly as you did the leash but move farther away. By looping the line to the side as you move away from the dog, you will keep him from becoming entangled in it. It is best, at this stage, not to attempt to reel in the line as he comes to you, since this will keep both hands employed so that you cannot give the hand signal.

When you have your dog coming to you quickly and without hesitation when you speak the *"Spot, Come!"* command, combine it with the *"Sit!"* As he comes up, and when he is directly in front of you and *close*, give him the *"sit"* command so that he comes in on the recall and sits in front of you.

Correcting Faults in the Recall

Should your dog evince a nonchalant attitude toward the recall, if he ambles slowly toward you instead of coming in with the snap and interest he should display, then it will be necessary to reel in the rope as he comes so that you can keep it taut and aid him to a faster pace by quick, sharp tugs on the line. Meanwhile move backward, away from the dog. You may find that you will have to step backward away from him in quick steps to make him follow with increasing alacrity.

Once a dog has broken the

66

Training to "Come!"

"Stay!" command, as he must to obey the recall, he may break prematurely and begin to follow you as soon as you step away from him. Reproach him with *"No!"* and make him remain at the *"Stay!"* until you give him the *"Come!"* command. When you face him to give the latter command, wait a few seconds, holding him in the *"Stay!"* command, before you counteract it with the recall signal. Move a few paces to the left, then to the right before you return directly in front of him and release him from the *"Stay!"* with the new recall command.

Remember that your dog's eyesight is not comparable to his hearing or sense of smell, so when you call him in from a distance it is best not to give a hand signal. He may confuse it with a visual signal used by you for one of the other commands. Use the oral command only and, after he works properly to it, there is no reason for you to shout it. His auditory ability is much greater than any human's.

This shouting of commands as it is taught by many obedience trainers to be emulated by their human pupils who, in turn, use it upon their own animals to enforce obedience, is not at all necessary or desirable. Only at the beginning of training should the trainer's voice be fairly loud. Each command must be expressed distinctly and with good diction so that it can be understood by the pupil and differentiated from other commands. As the dog becomes more familiar with the commands and works quickly, surely, and smoothly to obey, the trainer's voice can be appreciatively lowered until all orders are issued in an easy, but distinct, conversational tone.

Combining Commands

By combining all the lessons your dog has learned up to this point you can now take him through a very satisfactory pattern of obedience and extract from him a performance that is a glowing tribute to your ability as a trainer and to your pupil's mental competence.

Training to "Come!"

Beginning with the *"Sit!"* you move the dog off briskly in the *"Heel!"* position, executing several turns and figure eights. Finishing the *"Heel!"* your pupil *"sits"* again at your side. You now execute the *"Sit-stay!"* followed by the *"Down-stay!"* and, after moving around the dog to the side, back, and front to illustrate his sureness in the *"Stay!"* you return to his side and call him once again to the *"Sit!"* position. From *"Stay!"* in this position you move away from him for the recall when he will return to sit in front of you.

Now we must teach him the *"finish,"* which is nothing more or less than bringing him once again to the *"Sit!"* position at your left side.

The "Finish"

Your dog, after the recall, is sitting facing you and you must bring him around, facing in the same direction you are, and to your left side. To do so requires usage of the leash again. Hold the slack in your left hand and place your right hand, palm down, on the leash between you and your dog and, by pressure with your right hand, pull the animal toward your right. As you do this, step back with your right leg—leaving your left foot and leg in the position it was—and give the command, *"Spike, Heel!"* As you guide the dog behind you, his muzzle facing toward your left side, pass the leash from one hand to the other, behind, then in front, ending with it in your right hand, meanwhile bringing your right leg back to its former position beside your left leg.

As soon as the dog has reached the heel position on your left side, give him the command *"Sit!"* and the exercise is finished. This sounds much more complicated than it really is. Study the directions carefully for a few minutes, perhaps practice the movements without the dog so that you make no mistakes, and you will find the whole movement easy to execute.

The hardest part is to coax the pupil to move to the right and around your right leg to pass

Training to "Come!"

behind you. The whole exercise must be executed smoothly and fluidly without any hitches or hesitations in between. Let me caution you not to give the *"Heel!"* command in the *"finish"* too quickly. Allow the dog to sit in front of you for a few seconds before you issue the command for the *"finish"*. If you don't condition him to a definite pause between the front *"Sit!"* and the *"Heel!"* to *"finish,"* he will soon, of his own accord, eliminate the front *"sit,"* or give it only token recognition, and circle immediately into the *"Heel!"* position for the *"finish."*

Comments

The hand signal I advocated earlier in this chapter for use during the *"Come!"* was merely an added means of coaxing your dog to break the *"Stay!"* command. Later I explained that a dog, called from a distance, might confuse a hand signal for one accompanying another command since canine vision is limited. I personally use the

While your dog is in the sit-stay position, you can teach it to come to you on command. Such a command might save a dog's life.

hand signal developed in Germany for the recall which, when combined wih two other hand signals brings the *"finish"* to a neat close.

First use the oral command, *"King, Come!"* and, as the dog approaches you and reaches a point where his vision is clear and your movements easily seen by him, bring both palms up to your chest, elbows at your side, palms flat against your chest with fingers pointing upward toward your chin. Hit your chest with your palms to create a hollow sound as he comes in. Later, when he is letter perfect, you may eliminate the Tarzan beat and simply tap your chest with your palms.

With the dog heeding your palm-against-chest signal and therefore sitting before you, move your left hand, fingers pointing down, index finger extended, in a circling motion behind you, much as you moved your hand when you put pressure on the leash to bring him around you to the right for the *"finish."* Use the *"Heel!"* command with the hand motion.

When he has circled behind you and come to the *"Sit!"* position at heel at your left side, hold your left hand down, palm toward his nose, fingers extended and pointing toward the ground, in a stopping gesture directly in front of his face. To ulitize the last signal the leash must be passed from the left to the right hand.

By combining the visual (hand) and oral (voice) commands you are conditioning your dog to obey either (while, at the same time, bolstering and making more important the basic vocal commands). Later, with your dog working off leash, you will not be burdened with this important implement to early training and your dog will, after a while, react to only your hand signals if you wish him to do so.

During basic dog training it is important to make good use of the collar and leash. Later when the dog is conditioned to respond to the commands it has learned, the leash can be removed.

Basic Training Completed

You and your pupil are now on the training homestretch. As a matter of fact if you were to quit now you would, for all general purposes, have a very well trained and behaved canine citizen.

But we are going to add a bit of extra polish to our pupil's basic education and teach him to *Stand!"* and to *"Stand—stay!"* These commands, when learned, will help you to groom and wash your dog with greater ease and will be excellent training for the show ring should he prove to mature into a specimen of show caliber. This is also an exercise that is required in the obedience ring.

Many show people will tell you that it is not good to train your dog in obedience if you are going to show him. They seem, after much questioning, to object to the heeling-sit position which the trained animal takes when you come to a halt. With this new exercise we confound such objectors because we can, by giving the command, have the dog stand instead of sit. Another advantage found in training your

dog to this *"Stand!"* command is in basic cleanliness during inclement weather. If you are walking your dog during rainy or snowy weather and you stop to chat with a neighbor or friend, the *"Stand-stay!"* command will keep your dog from sitting down in mud or water and soiling his underparts.

Teaching to "Stand-stay"

Take your usual starting position with the dog at *"Sit!"* beside you. Begin to move ahead, giving the *"Heel!"* command. Then, as you come to the stop when your pupil ordinarily takes the *"Sit!"* position at your side, reach down quickly with your left hand, put it under his belly and hold him up (or keep him from sitting), issuing at the same time the command *"Stand!"* If you have followed directions from the beginning of the book, you will be aided in your endeavor by the early training you gave the puppy to stand while holding him at arm's length.

Basic Training Completed

Once you have made the dog obey the *"Stand!"* command, bring your palm down before his face, giving the command *"Stay!"* and stepping away from him. His posture may be deplorable, but do not attempt to correct it until he is perfect in reacting to the *"Stand-stay!"* command.

At this stage of his training it is necessary to bring in a third party, namely someone who will oblige you by walking around the dog, touching him here and there much as a show ring judge would do during examination in the conformation ring, while the animal, obeying your *"Stand-stay!"* command, stands rock-still.

When you return to the dog, give him the *"Stand-stay!"* command again so he will remain standing. His tendency will be to sit as soon as you reach his side. In this exercise the leash should be handled as little as possible. Merely allow it to hang with a comfortable slack during the whole performance.

When the lesson is learned, circle around him when you return as you did in the *"Sit-stay!"* and *"Down-stay!"* and touch him gently here and there. If he turns his head to look at you, push it back gently to face toward the front.

Commands Combined

Again, as you always have done, go through the whole routine of commands. Be sure your dog differentiates between the *"Sit-stay!"* and the *"Stand-stay!"* If you have your pupil in the *"Sit-stay!"* at your side and wish to give him the command *"Stand-stay!"* take a step or two forward to get him to a stand naturally before giving the command. About five sessions should perfect him.

Work with your dog, keeping the commands, and his conditioned reflexes to them, fresh. Take him with you when you go shopping or visiting so that he will learn to obey under different environmental circumstances.

After you are sure that your dog will obey any and all of the

Basic Training Completed

commands he has been taught by you smoothly and with perfection, then you must remove the leash and put him through the whole routine of exercises off leash and free.

Working off Leash

When you begin *"Heeling!"* your dog off leash, if he is tall enough at the shoulder, it is best to at first loop one finger in the circle of the chain choke collar for physical control. Lessen this control until your pupil is *"Heeling!"* free, naturally, and well.

Please do not rush into this phase of training. If you do you can very well ruin all that you have accomplished before. Be absolutely sure that your dog is ready to work off leash. If he still needs help on leash in any of the exercises or any small phase of them, he is not ready to work free. Your pupil must be an absolutely and completely reliable student on the leash before he can be allowed to work without it.

If possible it is the better part of valor to begin working your dog off leash in an enclosure where he can be easily captured should he prove less reliable than you thought. You must act relaxed and pretend that the dog is on leash and as completely under your control as he was before. Any uneasiness on your part will be conveyed to your dog and reflect in his behavior.

Generally speaking, you will find that working *off* leash presents no more problems than working *on* leash and I am sure that if you have followed instructions faithfully you will be very proud of your trained dog.

Just one word of caution here. Often dogs will work with less vigor and punctuality off leash. Do not allow it. Make your dog work with all the snap and accuracy he exhibited when on leash. It is very easy for either you or your animal to fall into sloppy behavior once the major part of his basic training is over. Examine yourself first if your pupil has lost his early spark in performance. Perhaps it is your attitude that is the cause.

Extra Training Bonuses

There are always a few more hints to give, a word or two more to say before talk on training is completed, advice that should be given about subjects not directly covered by general training, but important in canine deportment.

One of these yet-to-be-spoken-of problems is barking. Some dogs are noisy and bark at everything. It is their nature to do so, for they are members of a breed that is genetically noisy. Most owners want to control the barking of their dog so he will quit when told to do so. To accomplish this grasp the animal by the muzzle to hold his jaws together and give him the command, *"Quiet!"* uttered sharply. *"No!"* can also be used, but when you use it you are admonishing the dog for committing a misdemeanor and, in so doing you make him feel guilty for raising an alarm to protect you and your family and property. You want him to tell you when something is amiss or when someone is approaching. But you also want him to quit when he has done his duty and you give him the command to subside. For all these reasons the new command *"Quiet!"* is to be preferred to *"No!"* or *"Shame!"*

Remember, you may have to work a bit harder when it comes to breaking your dog of the annoying habit of jumping up on you or your friends (who will soon be your enemies if this canine deportment continues.) As previously noted, the best means of dealing with the problem is to firmly grasp the dog's front paws and place them on the ground, at the same time admonishing him with a sharp "No!" If you patiently and consistently follow this method of training, it shouldn't be long before your dog catches on.

Your dog has learned the *"Halt"* command during his training in heeling. You will find that later the usefulness of this command can be broadened to bring to a stop any activity the dog may be engaged in at the moment that you wish halted immediately.

If the *"Halt!"* command is learned well it will aid you immeasurably in controlling a

Extra Training Bonuses

dog that is off leash, has become panicked, and is running away. Sometimes a familiar command that gets through the fog of fright to his consciousness will stop him and bring him back to a modicum of control.

There is a trick that German trainers use on dogs who persist

After every training session, pet your dog and lavish it with praise for being a good student. The two of you might want to have a game of catch afterwards.

in running wild or away when released from the leash, and it works with a sort of animal magic. The dog who engages in such conduct does so fully conscious of the fact that, once he has put distance between you, you cannot reach him to chastise him for his misconduct. The trick is to prove him wrong and

to do this you must employ another chain choke collar which you will retain in your hand.

When the culprit has run off and heeds your commands to return not at all, you must throw the chain collar so that it strikes either very close to him or hits his hocks. His confident cockiness will fall immediately into shattered shards around him. You have done what he thought you were incapable of doing, reached him at a distance to punish him, and he will return on command, crestfallen and forever after in awe of your power.

In the house every dog should have a place to call his own where his bed is and where he can snooze in peace. This area should be referred to as his *"Place!"* and when you want the rascal out from under your feet for any good and valid reason, the command *"Place!"* should send him scuttling to that spot of sanctuary to stay until called. To train him is simply a matter of identifying this location by pointing to it and repeating the word, *"Place!"* Later you can

Extra Training Bonuses

command, *"Fido, go to your PLACE!"* and he will obey.

Some dogs are forever carrying sticks or other objects in their mouths or bringing them to you. If your dog enjoys this form of entertainment it will be easy to teach him to *"Fetch!"* Repeat this command each time he brings anything to your hand. Or throw a stick or other object and command him to *"Fetch!"* it. Most dogs of the hunting breeds are easily taught this command as well as many individuals of other breeds. Later you can broaden this command to include the daily newspaper or your slippers, if you wish.

Jumping is another fun thing that most dogs like to do. To train them to do it upon command requires only that you join them when they jump, taking them over the jump with you and issuing the command, *"Jump!"* or *"Hup!"* if you prefer. In no time at all you will be able to direct your dog toward an obstacle and he will sail over it at your command, like a veteran steeplechaser. This exercise in jumping will pay

Your dog can be taught to fetch a variety of objects for you. You might want to start by having it retrieve a stick.

dividends later on if you wish to continue in obedience, particularly if you combine the object retrieving with the jumping.

You and your dog have now reached a point where you are a well-trained team. Take pride in your accomplishment and in the willingness and trainability of . your dog that made your accomplishment as a trainer possible. I have given you all the necessary fundamentals to make training your dog as easy as possible and, to have reached this page and the corresponding stage in training that it represents, you have evidently used everything written here to the best of

Extra Training Bonuses

advantage. If you wish to indulge in advance training you and your dog have as fine a training base as is possible and you can go on to any areas of training (within genetic and physical limits) you wish. The interesting world of canine training is your oyster. Good luck!

Part of obedience training for these dogs (above and below) has included retrieving an object over an obstacle.

Obedience Training and Trials

Within the area of obedience trial competition there are match shows for the neophyte which are extremely interesting, will allow you to meet other dog owners who, like yourself, are interested in training, and give both you and your dog that first taste of competition, but in an easy-to-take fashion. If you are lucky (or competent) you may also win a small (but always cherished) trophy in these informal matches. Such competitions will probably whet your appetite for more exciting and difficult obedience trials such as those which are held all over the United States under the auspices of the American Kennel Club. You perform under a judge who scores your dog according to its ability to perform the various exercises. There are four classes in these obedience trials: Novice, Open, Utility, and tracking.

The Novice Class

In the Novice Class the dog will be judged on the following basis:

TEST MAXIMUM SCORE
Heel on lead...............40
Stand for examination.......30
Heel free—off lead.........40
Recall (come on command)....30
One-minute sit (handler in ring)30
Three-minute down (handler in ring).....................30
Maximum total score......200

If the dog "qualifies" in three shows by earning at least 50% of the points for each test, with a total of at least 170 for the trial, he has earned the Companion Dog degree and the letters C.D. (Companion Dog) are entered after his name in the American Kennel Club records.

Open Class Competition

After the dog has earned his Companion Dog title, he is eligible to enter the Open Class competition and compete for his next degree. He will be judged on this basis:

TEST MAXIMUM SCORE
Heel free.................40
Drop on recall.............30
Retrieve (wooden dumbbell) on flat....................20

Obedience Training and Trials

Retrieve over obstacle (hurdle). 30
Broad jump 20
Three-minute sit (handler out of
   ring) 30
Five-minute down (handler out of
   ring) 30
Maximum total score 200

Again he must qualify in three shows for the C.D.X. (Companion Dog Excellent) title, earning at least 50% of the points for each test, with a total of at least 170 for the trial. He is then eligible to compete in the Utility Class, where he can earn the Utility Dog (U.D.) degree in these rugged tests:

Utility Dog Degree

After your dog has been awarded his C.D.X. he is eligible to compete in Utility Dog Competition. To enter here he must be, of necessity, a very finished performer as perusal of the tests involved will show.

TEST MAXIMUM SCORE
Scent discrimination
   (picking up article
   handled by master from group)

Article 1 30
Scent discrimination Article 2 . 30
Directed Retrieve 30
Signal exercise (heeling, etc., on
hand signal) 40
Directed jumping (over hurdle
   and bar jump) 40
Group examination 30
Maximum total score 200

Dogs that are disqualified from breed shows because of neutering or physical defects are eligible to compete in these trials. Besides the formal A.K.C. obedience trials, there are informal "match" trials in which dogs compete for ribbons and inexpensive trophies. These shows are run by many local fanciers' clubs and by all-breed obedience clubs. In many localities the humane society and other groups conduct their own obedience shows. Your local newspaper, pet shop proprietor or kennel club can keep you informed about such shows in your vicinity, and you will find them listed in the different dog magazines or in the pet column of your paper.

Index